LIVING ON PURPOSE

Living ON PURPOSE

30 DAYS IN THE BOOK OF JAMES

CATHY MADAVAN

CWR

Copyright © Cathy Madavan, 2018

Published 2018 by CWR, Waverley Abbey House, Waverley Lane, Farnham, Surrey
GU9 8EP, UK.

CWR is a Registered Charity – Number 294387 and a Limited Company registered in
England – Registration Number 1990308

The right of Cathy Madavan to be identified as the author of this work has been asserted
by her in accordance with the Copyright, Designs and Patents Act 1988.

All rights reserved. No part of this publication may be reproduced, stored in a retrieval
system or transmitted, in any form or by any means, electronic, mechanical,
photocopying, recording or otherwise, with the prior permission of CWR.

For a list of National Distributors, see www.cwr.org.uk/distributors

Unless otherwise indicated, all Scripture references are from the Holy Bible: New
International Version (NIV, Anglicised edition), copyright © 1973, 1978, 1984, 2011 by Biblica.

Concept development, editing, design and production by CWR.

Printed in the UK by Linney.

ISBN: 978-1-78259-829-9

To Mark – here's to 25 years of making it up as we go along, trying to live on purpose. What a wonderful learning curve it has been.

To my girls – it's an honour to be your Mum and to see you flourish. May God grant you courage and wisdom for the adventure ahead.

To my friends – what would life be without buddies and colleagues who love and laugh a lot? You're amazing.

To our church family – your faithfulness and bravery as we build together has been incredible. Can't wait to see what God will do.

CONTENTS

Foreword by Krish Kandiah   8
Introduction   10

Day 1 – Wisdom for living   12
Day 2 – Behind the scenes   14
Day 3 – Testing and trusting   16
Day 4 – Single-minded belief   18
Day 5 – A shared inheritance   20
Day 6 – Don't get dragged down   22

Abiding on purpose   **24**
Day 7 – Cultivating righteousness   30
Day 8 – Take a closer look   32
Day 9 – Caring for the least   34
Day 10 – God has no favourites   36
Day 11 – Keeping the royal law   38
Day 12 – Mercy above all   40

Serving on purpose   **42**
Day 13 – A balanced approach   48
Day 14 – Daring to trust   50
Day 15 – Recognising your responsibility   52
Day 16 – Taming the tongue   54
Day 17 – Praising and cursing   56
Day 18 – The wisdom of heaven   58

Loving on purpose   **60**

Day 19 – A battle within us   66

Day 20 – A jealous God   68

Day 21 – Greater grace   70

Day 22 – Lifting others up   72

Day 23 – A disappearing mist   74

Day 24 – Your stuff is not enough   76

Growing on purpose   **78**

Day 25 – Waiting well   84

Day 26 – You are not alone   86

Day 27 – Consistent and clear   88

Day 28 – Power-assisted living   90

Day 29 – Bringing people home   92

Day 30 – The beginning of wisdom   94

FOREWORD

My life has been transformed by the people I have had the privilege to spend time with. It's because I spent some time with some serious runners that I gained the inspiration to try and get fitter myself. It's because I spent some time with some extraordinary entrepreneurs that I had the courage to start my charity, Home for Good. It's because of my wife's compassion that we became a fostering family. It is because of the fostered children in my life that I am passionate about helping those who are vulnerable.

I expect you too can think of men and women who have made a positive impact in your life: those who have inspired you to live well for God, to dare greatly for the kingdom and to love more courageously. 'As iron sharpens iron, so one person sharpens another.' This is how it is put in Proverbs 27:17. Scripture itself affirms what we know instinctively – spending time with inspirational people can make us stronger, more useful, more focused.

This is why Cathy Madavan's book, *Living on Purpose*, is such a great idea. Through its pages we get to spend 30 days in the challenging company of someone who had grown up with Jesus – James. What an amazing thought! James was inspired by God to write a most powerful and relevant letter to God's people throughout the world. The Spirit of God has preserved this letter for us and it speaks as pertinently to us today as it did to its original audience two millennia ago. As we spend time with James we discover that he is uncompromising, blunt, radical and aggressive. But James is also wise, visionary, practical and faithful. My prayer for you as you linger in his company is that these same character traits would work their way into your life as you read the Word of God and dare to do what it says.

We so need wisdom and insight in order to live on purpose rather than drifting through life. We need firm foundations that will help us to build our life with God according to His instruction. This means treasuring great books and podcasts, inspired sermons, insightful friends and the many resources God has placed at our disposal. But, as the proverb above and the book of James will remind us in the coming days, wisdom is essentially us living out our faith obediently, following Jesus with determination and not forgetting or turning away from the truth we already know. Fortunately, James reveals plenty of the challenging but profound teaching that will indeed guide our paths, if we do not forsake what we hear.

Wise living then, does not happen by accident. This is a call to living on purpose. This is intentionally choosing to understand and apply what truly matters. This is about wholeheartedly embracing a disciplined but abundant life, where we discover that living in all its fullness begins as we fully surrender to God.

Thank You, Lord, for Your Word and for Your wisdom that watches over me. Fill me with Your Spirit and Your understanding, as I seek to follow You faithfully on purpose. Amen.

BEHIND THE SCENES

JAMES 1:1

'James, a servant of God and of the Lord Jesus Christ, To the twelve tribes scattered among the nations: Greetings.'

In our lounge we have many mysterious black boxes sitting under our TV, with an equally baffling mountain of allegedly corresponding remote controls. One of these boxes, however, is very useful. It is one of those clever TV recorders where you store series after series of programmes in the unrealistic hope that one day you will have time to watch any of them. It's a great gadget. But last week as I scrolled through menus trying to find something to watch, I realised something disturbing about myself: I am essentially a very nosey person who records endless shows about people's houses, people's workplaces and people's family histories. It seems I rather like getting behind the scenes, under the surface and into the nooks and crannies of the lives of other people, without having to actually deal with their messy lives in person. I think I may have issues.

Perhaps though, this natural 'curiosity' explains why I am so drawn to the book of James. This letter is not some carefully curated Instagram account of the Early Church or a glossy party political broadcast. This is a raw, honest and sometimes brutally direct letter instructing the early Christians about how to live out their faith on purpose in a tough culture.

But what particularly piques my interest is the person behind the letter, the author who lifts the lid on the issues of the day. The author of the book of James is not James (son of Zebedee) the disciple of Jesus; rather it is James, who according to most commentators and scholars was almost certainly Jesus' brother. As a close relative, James would have known Jesus in a very particular and personal way. He would have seen Jesus develop and grow into the man God intended Him to be. James would have weighed up His claims to be the Messiah; he would have known about the miracles and that He had died for His convictions. James would have come to terms with the implications of the empty tomb and been convinced by the truth of Jesus when Jesus appeared to him personally (1 Cor. 15:7). After the death of Jesus, James became a significant figure as leader of the church in Jerusalem, and was a man clearly respected for his insight into the practical realities of living as a follower of Christ.

How wonderful for us to have this behind the scenes recording of events and issues affecting the Early Church. How fascinating to read James' teaching and to sense his heartfelt passion for God's people. But, make no mistake, as we get up close and personal to somebody who knew Jesus so well, he will continue to lift the lid on the issues in our lives too. His desire for Jesus' followers to stay focused and to remain faithful, even against the odds, is still as relevant as ever.

Thank You, God, for the truth of the life, death and resurrection of Jesus. Thank You for the hope I find in You. As I go deeper into Your Word, may I know You more than ever before. Amen.

TESTING AND TRUSTING

JAMES 1:2-4

'Consider it pure joy, my brothers and sisters, whenever you face trials of many kinds, because you know that the testing of your faith produces perseverance. **Let perseverance finish its work so that you may be mature and complete, not lacking anything.'**

First impressions are important. We are told that within minutes of meeting others, we will have made conclusions about their personality and whether we like them based on what they say and how they say it. Apparently, we form a kind of gut instinct about people almost instantaneously. Well, there's no getting away from it: this letter from James certainly makes a distinct first impression. It does not begin with any kind of social chit-chat or gushing praise. There are no pastoral niceties or pietistic platitudes from this church leader. Not even close. In fact, he steps straight into how our attitude to suffering determines our maturity. James urges us to joyfully allow perseverance to do its work in us.

James is certainly direct, but he is also very wise. He knew very well that we all face battles – between the habits of our old nature and our new nature, but also as we navigate life's unexpected twists and turns. As Alec Motyer once said, 'Christians are a special people, but not a protected species.'*

The issue then, is not *whether* we will face trials but *how* we choose to *respond* during these tough times. This is critical to whether we will grow to be 'mature and complete'. When we are up against it, do we pull back or push through? Do we retreat from God and others, or accept that perseverance, patience and prayer are all part of the deal as we develop our spiritual muscles? In fact, Jesus – our role model and the 'author of salvation' – was Himself made perfect through suffering (Heb. 2:10).

I don't know where you feel tested right now, but every season of life seems to bring its own trials. I can look back on times of crippling insecurity, loneliness, divorcing parents, my husband's scary diagnosis, sleepless nights, toddler tantrums, teenage traumas and fears about so many things. And while I don't think I have often (OK, ever) risen to feeling 'joy' in these trials, I do gain enormous satisfaction from knowing that God has been with me and has given me resilience as I have persevered through the process with Him.

So, rather than praying that we never suffer (which is unrealistic at best and holy denial at worst!), James encourages us to embrace the valleys as well as the mountains. Life might not get easier, but we can get stronger knowing that Jesus is victorious and He is with us. Trusting our Saviour during the testing times will lead to sacred moments of grace and a hope beyond compare.

Heavenly Father, I confess I don't always find life easy but I surrender my heart and mind to You. I pray I might know more of Christ in His suffering as I face my own challenges. Holy Spirit, work in me to make me 'mature and complete' and help me to show Jesus to those who are struggling now. Amen.

*Alec Motyer, *The Message of James* (Westmont, IL, USA: IVP Academic, 1985)

SINGLE-MINDED BELIEF

JAMES 1:5-8

'If any of you lacks wisdom, you should ask God, who gives generously to all without finding fault, and it will be given to you. **But when you ask, you must believe and not doubt, because the one who doubts is like a wave of the sea, blown and tossed by the wind.** *That person should not expect to receive anything from the Lord. Such a person is double-minded and unstable in all they do.'*

Suddenly it seems I am a parent of older children. It's strange since I am sure they were in preschool only yesterday. Apparently, time has moved on and I am now one of those people I thought were oh-so-old when I had toddlers grabbing hold of my legs. One of the many things I didn't realise back then was how much teenagers still need their parents. It has rather taken me by surprise, to be honest. At the most inopportune moments there are emergency CAPS LOCK texts asking for critical documents or tear-filled phone calls as exam stress takes its toll. And I've noticed that older children still regularly ask their parents for two things: money and advice. They always take the money…

Seriously though, I am grateful that our children still ask us for our input and prayers. We love supporting them and talking with them. And, in the same way that asking parents or trusted friends for advice is usually a good move, asking God for wisdom is always an excellent idea. We simply cannot work out everything on our own. But just as teenagers don't immediately light up at the wisdom of their extraordinarily insightful parents, we are sometimes a little reticent in our receptiveness to our heavenly Father as well.

Likewise, James tells us that the crown of life, new birth and every good thing is found when we persevere on God's upward path of life, even (and especially) when it is hard going. This is so true. The greatest vistas, the deepest friendships, the most wonderful accomplishments, the lasting spiritual fruit are all found as we purposefully choose to keep our eyes focused above the challenges to follow the upward call of Christ.

But in verse 14 (and James pulls no punches here), we are told what we already know but don't want to admit: we can all be so easily dragged downhill by our own desires. Let's be honest, going downhill is no bother at all, and temptation really wouldn't be temptation if it wasn't attractive in some way. But greed, gossip, laziness, pride or lust are simply not paths that ultimately lead to God's promised blessing.

James was a passionate pastor who wanted to keep the Church on track within a turbulent culture, even if that meant confronting tough issues. That's why he tells his 'dear brothers and sisters' not to be deceived. He cares about them, and as one involved in church leadership myself, I totally understand his concern. It is a tragedy when lives and families are messed up because the downhill option seemed easier or more attractive at the time.

The truth is, we will all face tests and trials as well as great opportunities – and with these things come temptation. If we don't take responsibility for our own motives and actions (instead of blaming God, others or our circumstances), then we might feel justified or comfortable on the downward path for a while, but it won't compare to receiving the crown of life that Jesus longs to give us.

Search my heart, Lord, and reveal to me where I am deceived, misguided or blind to my own sin. Lead me today on Your upward path of truth, righteousness and blessing. Amen.

Abiding

Last summer, our family went on holiday to a house belonging to some special friends. This couple very generously allowed us to stay in their home with its beautiful coastal views so that we could enjoy some much-needed peace and quiet away from normal busy life. We loved it. We completed jigsaw puzzles, played games, went for walks, read books, ate lots of food and generally had a wonderful time. For transparency's sake, I should clarify that there was not tranquillity and harmony each moment of every day and not everybody was begging to go for walks with me in the drizzle. There were some challenging moments (hello family life), but there were also wonderful memories made as we snuggled on the veranda watching shooting stars and sat eating ice creams together on the harbour wall.

But as much as we felt relaxed and welcome, that lovely house was never our *home*. At the end of the day, we were just visitors. It wasn't our permanent place. We couldn't start painting the walls or moving the furniture around. We didn't remodel their kitchen or landscape the garden. That would be a bit rude. So, as those two lovely weeks ended, we returned to our own house, where despite the lack of sea view and even with the mounting pile of laundry, we knew we had arrived home. This is our place. This is where long-term life happens, even when it is messy. This is where forgiveness is regularly dispensed and daily challenges are faced together. This is where we can remodel what needs changing and refurbish what needs a new lease of life. This is the place where I can rearrange cushions until my little heart is content (everybody needs a hobby, OK?) and where we can welcome people into a place shaped by our values and our way of doing things. This is home. This is where we dwell and kick off our shoes. We abide here.

There really is no place like home. Dorothy knew this when she was in Oz, and we know it too. Feeling that we have a place called home is important for our security and wellbeing, and not having a safe place where we may belong can be hugely detrimental. Every refugee and child needs a loving place to call home, as Krish Kandiah and the charity 'Home for Good' so poignantly ask us to consider. But beyond the necessity of a physical home, our soul also aches for a place to dwell. The writer of the book of Hebrews tells us that 'this world is not our permanent home; we are looking forward to a home yet to come' (Heb. 13:14, NLT). We are visitors here. This life is temporary and our desire for home is an echo of our yearning to be welcomed into our eternal dwelling place.

There will be some phases of life where we will feel more 'at home' than others. Even today, some of us will feel like we are in transit, restless, displaced and struggling with discomfort of some kind or another. Others of us are currently in a peaceful place where we can admire the view and breathe deeply. We all travel through these different seasons in different ways. But ultimately there is a place where we are always unconditionally accepted and where we are welcomed just as we are. God's presence is our glorious permanent home and eternity with Him will be our infinite place of residence, where pain and sickness are left at the door and where love and justice furnish every room more beautifully than we can imagine. In Him we find our home.

This is why Jesus takes His disciples to a vine and clearly tells them to abide in Him, before He takes His final journey to the cross (John 15:1–5). He knew that every believer needs to remember where they belong and to deliberately stay grafted into His goodness. The default setting of the human heart, ever since the Garden of Eden, has been to try and nourish ourselves and isolate ourselves from our maker. We somehow believe our own efforts or success will create the fulfilment and peace we so eagerly desire, but this is only ever satisfied as we find rest in Him. Those first disciples would have known that growing and maintaining a vine takes an enormous amount of effort and discipline; it takes year-round training and pruning and shaping and grafting for a vine to stay strong and fruitful. Likewise, staying close to Jesus takes care and attention. We need to abide in Him on purpose, as He is the source of life and of *our* purpose, which is to grow fruit.

Perhaps, like me, you need to make yourself more at home with your heavenly Father. Regularly, I am pulled forcefully into the vortex of to-do lists, tasks and low-level anxiety about what I need to get done, that if left unchecked, I revert to my own default of striving and independence. It's like I think that with enough effort I can produce my own fruit, unattached to the vine. Honestly, I will often abide in stress. I also easily abide in hard work. I naturally abide in busyness. Which all goes to explain why abiding with me is rather hard work (just ask my husband).

Isn't it time to come back to this instruction from Jesus? Abiding in God, deliberately dwelling in His presence and loving Him above everything else should surely be our goal and our place of peace. Success, wealth, significance and busyness are false gods, and choosing to set up our tent in their camp is never going to satisfy us. Likewise, choosing to live in disappointment, rejection and isolation will never lead to freedom. We are called to dwell in the land of hope. We are invited to abide in the presence of God and to remain in His love so that He can remain in us, wherever we are and whatever our circumstances.

Everything we need flows from abiding in God's presence. We have been created to worship Him. Some of us are so busy spinning that we don't ever rest in His presence long enough to really know we are home. Others of us have established a healthier rhythm but still need to practise being in His presence as we do life in the business meeting or at the supermarket. The wonderful truth is that we don't ever have to leave home when we abide in God. We don't just visit His presence for a holiday or a refreshing retreat. He isn't only to be found at a festival, on a Sunday morning or in our quiet time, as important as those places are. God never leaves but sadly we often leave Him.

So, as we come home again to our heavenly Father today, He welcomes us, sets the table for us, stills our hearts and invites us to abide in His presence. It is up to us to make ourselves fully at home and to purposefully dwell in the place we long for. His presence is our perfect home.

• What separates you from the vine? How often do you abide in independence or rejection, for example? Read John 15 again and allow God to speak to you.

• Do you feel settled or displaced in your current circumstances? Are there some areas where you feel you are being 'pruned' or where you need extra help? How can your experiences draw you back into the vine so that you can draw on God's strength?

• What does 'home' mean for you? Have you ever longed for a place that felt like the home of your imagination?

• Does knowing your eternity is in God's presence shape how you live today? What reminders or habits would help you to be more fully aware of your ultimate home wherever you are?

• How can we help others to discover that there is no place like home? Are there practical ways by which we might welcome others into God's presence and into His family?

Imagine being welcomed into the most beautiful home you have ever seen, where a room has already been prepared in advance for you. The table is laden with your favourite food and peace, joy and laughter permeate the air. You live here. Let it sink in. Take some time to make yourself at home in God's presence today.

CULTIVATING RIGHTEOUSNESS

'My dear brothers and sisters, take note of this: Everyone should be quick to listen, slow to speak and slow to become angry, because human anger does not produce the righteousness that God desires. **Therefore, get rid of all moral filth and the evil that is so prevalent and humbly accept the word planted in you, which can save you.'**

Every year, I optimistically decide to replant the small area of our garden dedicated to growing vegetables. With lofty ambitions, I spend a fortune at my local garden centre on plugs of tomatoes, broccoli and beans before returning home to painstakingly plant them into neat, labelled rows. Then, as I sit back and admire my patch of horticultural brilliance, I imagine myself picking my bountiful home-grown harvest and serving them to my adoring friends and family while fending off the compliments from all who admire my endeavours.

Sadly, this never, ever happens. The reality is that each year my poorly prepared soil and impatient nature, combined with a total lack of care, create the perfect environment for enormous weeds to flourish while my tender little plants wither and die. It's all rather humiliating.

Today's verses are an absolute masterclass in how to cultivate the right things. James encourages us to 'humbly accept the word planted in [us]' (v21). As we receive God's forgiveness, read Scripture and dwell in His presence, we are effectively planting potential for a spiritual abundance which will nourish us and bring life to others.

But that is not enough, James says. We must then diligently

polluted by the world and its priorities. Consumerism is the cultural religion of the day in the developed world and a filter through which we see almost everything. When considering their time, their relationships and even their prayer life or church life, many people wonder 'what is in it for me?' rather than 'what can I give here?' Often, we'd like everything to meet our needs and to be of the highest quality but we don't offer to make a commitment or difference ourselves.

This is not the way of the gospel. Jesus saw widows and orphans, the oppressed and the distressed and consistently spoke words of life and acted to bring about change. His 'religion' always expressed itself in caring for others, bringing hope and salvation. Jesus' beliefs didn't ever stay wrapped up in good intentions but worked themselves out into His life: giving of Himself for the benefit of others – ultimately sacrificing His life.

Thankfully, this is something we can all grow in, and Jesus' trustworthy promise is that He will always be with us as we seek to deliberately live out our faith, serving and caring for those in need.

Show me, Lord, how to live out what I believe. Fill me with Your compassion for those in need and help me to follow You in what I do as well as what I say. Amen.

GOD HAS NO FAVOURITES

'My brothers and sisters, believers in our glorious Lord Jesus Christ must not show favouritism.
Suppose a man comes into your meeting wearing a gold ring and fine clothes, and a poor man in filthy old clothes also comes in. If you show special attention to the man wearing fine clothes and say, "Here's a good seat for you," but say to the poor man, "You stand there" or "Sit on the floor by my feet," have you not discriminated among yourselves and become judges with evil thoughts? Listen, my dear brothers and sisters: has not God chosen those who are poor in the eyes of the world to be rich in faith and to inherit the kingdom he promised those who love him? But you have dishonoured the poor. Is it not the rich who are exploiting you? Are they not the ones who are dragging you into court? Are they not the ones who are blaspheming the noble name of him to whom you belong?'

My first attempts at preaching began soon after I became a Christian at university, before I knew much about what theology was or who wrote what in which Testament. It's fair to say that my enthusiasm has compensated for a great deal of ignorance over the years, although I have learned much along the way. Like me though, I am sure you are deeply grateful for the wonderful teachers and communicators who bring the truth to life in compelling ways. James was certainly a great preacher. Can't you just hear him telling this story about the rich man who swaggers into church wearing his finery, while the stewards prepare the finest seat for him? Then he skilfully contrasts this with the man who is literally filthy, and the very different treatment he receives.

James' point about favouritism is very clear as he draws us into the scene. But it's also worth noticing how he begins this whole illustration with the backdrop of the 'glorious Lord Jesus Christ' (v1). He reminds his fellow believers that Jesus is richer and filled with more splendour than any human being could ever be, but He lived on earth in the kind of humble conditions that, as His brother, James knew only too well. This bigger perspective reminds us that every human is of equal value before our majestic Saviour; there is completely level ground at the foot of the cross.

This passage might provoke us to ask: why do we still favour people with status, a million twitter followers or a massive bank balance, when the currency of faith is the same for us all? Why do wealthier churches and high profile Christians get so much more attention than those working behind the scenes in the most challenging places? Why do we still get dazzled by those with power, even though we are far more likely to be exploited by the rich? The poor have so much to teach us, yet who are we most likely to want to impress or learn from?

Remember, James is saying, Jesus really does not have any favourites and if anything, His heart always leans towards the poor. He had a choice, after all, about turning up in a palace or a stable, and it was the stable that won. This descriptive teaching is a challenging wake up call for all of us about our attitudes and preferential treatment of certain people, but it is also a call to purposefully look past our first impressions; to see people as God sees them. As it says in 1 Samuel 16:7: 'People look at the outward appearance, but the LORD looks at the heart.'

Show me, Lord, where I try to impress or get approval from influential people. Help me to see past the superficial, to see and love all people as You do. Amen.

KEEPING THE ROYAL LAW

JAMES 2:8–11

'If you really keep the royal law found in Scripture, "Love your neighbour as yourself," you are doing right. But if you show favouritism, you sin and are convicted by the law as lawbreakers. **For whoever keeps the whole law and yet stumbles at just one point is guilty of breaking all of it.** *For he who said, "You shall not commit adultery," also said, "You shall not murder." If you do not commit adultery but do commit murder, you have become a lawbreaker.'*

When I was young, my idea of a treat was going to Woolworths to get a bag of pick and mix sweets. For those too young to remember (yeah, yeah, whatever), back in the seventies the average ten-year-old was not banging on about a new smart phone or tickets to a pop concert that cost more than an armchair. No, we were busy eating our synthetic mashed potato and watching Grange Hill, unaware of how simple our lives really were. For me, a trip to Woolworths was 'properly' exciting. What could be better than stuffing a bag with your favourite sweets while avoiding those weird fluffy pink prawns and pretend white chocolates? I would fill up that bag with gummy eggs, milk bottles, liquorice swirls and long luscious strawberry laces. Paradise.

But what is an ideal scenario for sweets is not so desirable for Christian beliefs. It's just not possible to have a pick and mix theology that selects the values we like while ditching the things that don't taste so good to us. James, talking here both about favouritism but also discipleship generally, says that you can't live congratulating yourself for not committing one sin when you're quite happy indulging in another. Jesus is either

Lord of all or He is not Lord at all, as the saying goes.

Sometimes we reassure ourselves by looking around at others, thinking that compared to their selfishness or their big moral failure, we can give ourselves a slightly smug pat on the back. Or conversely, we look at other people's spirituality and blessing and feel like lowly worms who don't seem to be able to follow God with any consistency at all. But life is not a competition; life is a pilgrimage. Together we seek to live out the 'Royal Law' which James uses here, weaving the Old and New Testaments together, as he reminds us to love our King and our neighbour wholeheartedly and faithfully.

Being called to follow Jesus in every area of life is not easy, but He never asks us to do what we cannot do by His power. With His help, we can choose a holy life which will lead to faith adventures beyond all we could ask or imagine (see Eph. 3:20). We miss out on God's best for us when we limit our faith to just the bits we like; we need to love all people, not just those with whom we would naturally mingle. So, as we purposefully pick up our faith and mix with one another, we will, with the Spirit's empowering, indeed taste and see that the Lord is always good and will never let us down.

Heavenly Father, forgive my inconsistency and my tendency to justify my own actions. Help me to follow You in every area of life, and show me where to trust You further. Amen.

MERCY ABOVE ALL

JAMES 2:12-13

'Speak and act as those who are going to be judged by the law that gives freedom, because **judgment without mercy will be shown to anyone who has not been merciful. Mercy triumphs over judgment.'**

If people had to come up with one word to describe you, what would it be? In the lead-up to big projects or busy family seasons like Christmas and holidays, my family might choose the word 'frenzied' to describe me. I become a bit of a focused stress-monster as I tackle my to-do lists, planning each day with military precision. Hopefully though, for most of the year, they might find a word with more positive connotations. I'm in denial. Humour me.

Similarly, if you asked people to choose just one word to describe God, how would they respond? It would probably depend on their theological understanding and their own experience, and, of course, it's not easy to summarise the creator of the universe into a soundbite anyway. James however, forever the concise communicator, encapsulates some of God's attributes for us here in a challenging but reassuring few words.

'Mercy triumphs over judgment', says James. Yes, God is holy but He also shows us mercy that outweighs His judgment. How wonderful. But these verses also remind us that we are accountable for our words and actions before God, which is worth considering perhaps more than we do. We are required to be disciples who demonstrate God's character by allowing our mercy to triumph over judgment as well. James says that if we want to be shown mercy, we also need to show mercy. Of course, we know we are forgiven and reconciled to God because of the sacrifice of Jesus, but we don't just get off the hook and continue to behave in whatever way we would like. Our holy and just God is looking for us to demonstrate His grace to others, and James seems to be saying that God takes it seriously when we don't.

Mercy then, should always be the trump card we play over judgment. It's all too easy to judge others, to stereotype, to make assumptions and to withhold blessing or forgiveness in so many ways. Our default position is often to judge. But we are called to be more like Christ in how we respond. To purposefully live mercifully. Just as God has been so kind and gracious to us, so that should be the measure we use with others. Our heavenly Father is not pleased when we withhold what He has generously given to us.

So, just as we might choose the wonderful word 'merciful' to describe God, hopefully that same word could be used to describe us as well. Let's pray that His mercy shines like a bright light in a dark sky of judgment through us and His Church today.

What do You and Your word say about me, Lord? Do I need to ask for forgiveness about being judgmental towards others? How can I be known for love and mercy today? Show me, I pray. Amen.

Serving

I recently read a fascinating article about the television show *Strictly Come Dancing*. Apparently, every season has consistently attained sky-high viewing figures, demonstrating the British public's long-standing commitment to fake tan and fancy footwork on telly. It seems that many of us are riveted by the astonishing commitment of these celebrities who are desperate to join the show and to learn how to become dancers in front of millions of people. It's a winning combination – the musicians are world-class, the set is extraordinary, the costumes are dazzling and the participants are a genuine demonstration of how hard work and a shedload of sequins can transform your life.

But the article didn't stop there. It went on to say that while the viewing figures of *Strictly* have continued to smash records, the number of people participating in real-life dance activity across the country has plummeted to an all-time low. How depressing. It seems that we are very happy to sit munching pizza on our sofas, watching couples doing the Charleston or Viennese Waltz – we see the value in it, we appreciate the progress and marvel at the end result, but we would prefer not to be the ones actually doing it, thank you very much.

Such is life. We have probably all admired successful business people or exceptional leaders and marvelled at their lifestyle and opportunities, but few of us would be prepared to make the sacrifices or to take the risks necessary to get to that position ourselves. We see athletes

- What stops you from being more wholehearted in your serving? Are there ways of overcoming some of these obstacles or attitudes? Pray about these issues.

- Acknowledging the limitations of your current circumstances, how could you step out in faith and discover more of God working through you? Are your talents and time being invested in wise and purposeful ways?

- What areas of social injustice or need breaks your heart? Where has God given you a passion for change? Are there steps you could take to make a difference?

A BALANCED APPROACH

JAMES 2:14-19

'*What good is it, my brothers and sisters, if someone claims to have faith but has no deeds? Can such faith save them? Suppose a brother or a sister is without clothes and daily food. If one of you says to them, "Go in peace; keep warm and well fed," but does nothing about their physical needs, what good is it? In the same way, faith by itself, if it is not accompanied by action, is dead.*
But someone will say, "You have faith; I have deeds." Show me your faith without deeds, and I will show you my faith by my deeds. *You believe that there is one God. Good! Even the demons believe that—and shudder.*'

Back in the day, when my husband and I were in our early twenties, we attended a training day where we took one of those personality tests (which you either love or hate). The idea was that it would help us in our ministry and our marriage. It certainly made an impact. In one exercise, we had to write for five minutes about a ship before comparing our work with each other. Mark had described the ship in minute detail, listing the measurements of mast heights with thorough explanations of the various crew roles. This, I realised, was what life would be like in a world without adjectives. I, however, created an imaginative (and some might say rather fabulous) story massively overloaded with description about an elegant galleon being tossed over tumultuous waves. We are *definitely* different. It is no surprise then that we both explore and express our faith quite differently too. Although we are both very focused individuals, my husband is more analytical and methodical, whereas I am more instinctive and creative. We each have our strengths and weaknesses as a result – as they say, 'teamwork makes the dream work'.

James, in this very well-known passage, illustrates what a balanced faith is and is not, whatever our natural predispositions might be. It is not enough to have a heartfelt emotional reaction to those in need but then to do nothing practical in response. Our feelings of compassion or good wishes do not help anybody unless we translate them into deeds. But likewise, it is not enough to rationally believe or to intellectually understand Scripture, while assuming others, more gifted at being 'nice', will take care of the response.

Faith must be expressed in how we live, whoever we are – practical, prophetic, academic, introvert or extrovert. By the way, James is not saying we are saved by these works instead of by grace or somehow degrading saving faith, as some might suggest. No, he is simply condemning a faith that is not expressed in loving deeds, which both Paul and Jesus' teaching would wholeheartedly support (Matt. 25:41–46). 'In other words, we are not saved *by* good works, but we are saved *for* good works.'*

Let's pray that our churches and our own lives (whatever our personality) will be hallmarked by both a renewed love of study and biblical theology, and a heartfelt commitment to social action and compassionate acts of kindness. This is the kind of balanced and authentic faith that James is commending and that our world so desperately needs.

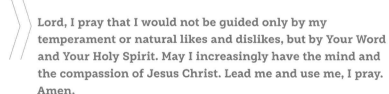

Lord, I pray that I would not be guided only by my temperament or natural likes and dislikes, but by Your Word and Your Holy Spirit. May I increasingly have the mind and the compassion of Jesus Christ. Lead me and use me, I pray. Amen.

*Thanks to Krish Kandiah for this helpful phrase, which is found in *Only the Brave: Determined discipleship* (Oxford: Lion Hudson, 2018), p67

DARING TO TRUST

JAMES 2:20–26

'You foolish person, do you want evidence that faith without deeds is useless? Was not our father Abraham considered righteous for what he did when he offered his son Isaac on the altar? You see that his faith and his actions were working together, and his faith was made complete by what he did. And the scripture was fulfilled that says, **"Abraham believed God, and it was credited to him as righteousness," and he was called God's friend. You see that a person is considered righteous by what they do and not by faith alone.** *In the same way, was not even Rahab the prostitute considered righteous for what she did when she gave lodging to the spies and sent them off in a different direction? As the body without the spirit is dead, so faith without deeds is dead.'*

Are you a person who likes to take risks, or do you prefer to stay nice and safe? Last year my brave (but nuts) husband jumped out of a plane to raise money for our church building project. This would be scary enough for anybody, but he has the added factor of being blind. Imagine the level of trust required in his instructor as he plunged thousands of feet into the unknown. My daughter, on the other hand, won't even try a new drink. Why would she bother attempting any new beverage when she already knows she likes apple juice? Taking risks is not so easy for her. And yet she has gradually learned to trust and to step out into the unfamiliar when necessary (and when bribed by her parents to do so).

As James continues his explanation of how authentic faith is demonstrated, he reminds us of two Old Testament characters who could not be more different: Abraham and Rahab. A patriarch and a prostitute, respected and disrespected, faithful and foreigner, Jew and Gentile. And yet both took extraordinary risks because of their faith, stepping out in bold obedience to follow God. We will never know exactly how hard it was for them or how courageous they needed to be to step out, but we know the result of their actions. Their daring belief that God could be trusted left a legacy of faith passed down through generations.

As Christians, we are saved by grace through faith, because Jesus held nothing back on the cross, humbly emptying Himself out for our forgiveness (Phil. 2:7–8). This was, and is, the ultimate demonstration that faith and action are inseparable. Nothing we can do in response will earn us salvation bonus points or will substitute the atoning sacrifice of Jesus. But, as Jesus always showed, faith and works, believing and doing, are part of the same deal, and comfortable risk-free Christianity is an entirely misguided and man-made invention. If we want to make our faith complete, then we are all called to respond to God as Abraham, Rahab and so many other biblical role models did. If we want to avoid faith-drift or spiritual sagginess, we too need to be intentional disciples who put our faith and worship into practice. Courageous faith is never a coincidence: it is a consequence of stepping out on purpose. We too need to be prepared to take risks, living a distinctive and daring life of faith and trust, where we don't just say we live for Christ, but we *do* it.

Thank You, Lord Jesus, for Your amazing grace. Thank You for biblical men and women who demonstrated their faith even when they were unsure of their future. May I live bravely and wholeheartedly for You today. Amen.

RECOGNISING YOUR RESPONSIBILITY

JAMES 3:1-2

'Not many of you should become teachers, my fellow believers, because you know that we who teach will be judged more strictly. *We all stumble in many ways. Anyone who is never at fault in what they say is perfect, able to keep their whole body in check.'*

I was fortunate enough to be a school governor for a while, and therefore spent a great deal of time with talented and committed teachers who were very aware of the power of their words. They knew that their vocabulary and their tone of voice were tools to use carefully and wisely, as every phrase had the potential to build up or inadvertently tear down a child.

Just as a schoolteacher takes their responsibility seriously, so those of us who teach the Bible have a special and challenging calling. James launches this memorable chapter about the tongue by highlighting those who teach in church.

Of course, in James' day every Jewish mother would have loved her precious son to be a Rabbi – it was a respected calling accompanied by status and popularity. A teacher of the law would have been a worthwhile and wonderful aspiration for any young person. Today, things are a little different. Often, there are not enough men or women entering training to lead our churches. Sadly, many congregations struggle to find committed volunteers willing to help run a church or to bring Scripture to life in small groups, junior church and youth clubs. God needs us to identify and empower this gifting within ourselves and in others – if it is the truth that sets us free then we need inspiring people to help us live in that freedom. Maybe God is asking some of us to step up and be willing to teach, whatever our perceived imperfections. It is a good idea to be more grateful for those who do help us to grapple with Scripture. It's important that we pray for them and encourage them however we can. It might be a privilege to lead or teach, but it is also a very real responsibility.

But while not everybody stands behind a lectern, we all have influence. Our whole life speaks. We are all needed if we are to support and invest in the next generation; we are all called to be faith role models and we should all help each other to understand and apply the Bible's teaching. And, of course, we all use words – on social media, in conversation and in our homes and workplaces, where we are called to be wise disciples who purposefully lift others up with words of life and truth. Our words matter, and how we say them matters too. Every one of us is a teacher of what it means to be a Christian today wherever God places us.

What an incredible honour. We might be far from perfect, but we are still called to share the amazing truth of God's goodness with others.

Thank You, Lord, for faithful pastors, preachers, small group leaders, writers and those who help children and young people to know You and Your Word. Help me to share Your truth and love with others today. Amen.

TAMING THE TONGUE

JAMES 3:3-8

'When we put bits into the mouths of horses to make them obey us, we can turn the whole animal. Or take ships as an example. Although they are so large and are driven by strong winds, they are steered by a very small rudder wherever the pilot wants to go. **Likewise, the tongue is a small part of the body, but it makes great boasts. Consider what a great forest is set on fire by a small spark.** The tongue also is a fire, a world of evil among the parts of the body. It corrupts the whole body, sets the whole course of one's life on fire, and is itself set on fire by hell. All kinds of animals, birds, reptiles and sea creatures are being tamed and have been tamed by mankind, but no human being can tame the tongue. It is a restless evil, full of deadly poison.'

I can still clearly recall the day when a new red cardigan somehow smuggled itself into a load of white laundry. Now, I don't have anything against the colour pink per se, but I was not exactly thrilled to remove the clothes from the washing machine to discover they were all dyed a geranium hue. That red cardigan certainly made its presence felt, and not in a good way.

In today's verses, James warns us that just as one drop of red in a drum of whites can affect the whole load, one word of gossip or innuendo in a community or a church can corrupt or pollute a whole pool of people in no time at all. Perhaps you have seen the Second World War poster that read, 'Careless words cost lives', warning ordinary people that a slip of the tongue could advance the mission of the enemy with catastrophic results. Similarly, most of us can recall a time when a few careless words have caused incredible pain, effectively doing the enemy's work of creating division and distrust. A single sentence spoken within our family, our workplace, our school or even our church that tarnished us with condemnation, failure or disappointment is still remembered years later.

So, these verses are far more than a warning to simply bite our tongues occasionally. Rather, we are being taught here that small words have a big impact. As we purposefully learn to master our words, the knock-on effect is that we also master our entire selves and the forces that lead us into sin and selfishness.

This incredible wisdom from James is expressed in brilliant, memorable pictures. Just as a tiny bit in the mouth of a horse and a small rudder can keep enormous power under control, so our words, when they are tamed, can strengthen and direct our whole life. In contrast, if we let our tongue gush forth unedited and unfiltered consciousness from our brain, it is more like a wildfire that consumes us and others. Sounds like the truth to me.

The good news is that our words do have the potential to make a huge difference, not just in a bad way but also in a profoundly good way. As we discipline our tongue, we are choosing to bring our fickle hearts into line in the process, giving us focus and wisdom. As we surrender our verbal output, we allow the Holy Spirit to input into our thoughts so that we might release the prophetic potential in others. Your tongue might be small but, be wary: your words are powerful.

Lord God, I believe that my words are spiritually significant. Help me to tame my tongue and harness Your power in my life. May my words release Your purposes and potential in others. Amen.

PRAISING AND CURSING

JAMES 3:9-12

'With the tongue we praise our Lord and Father, and with it we curse human beings, who have been made in God's likeness. **Out of the same mouth come praise and cursing. My brothers and sisters, this should not be. Can both fresh water and salt water flow from the same spring?** My brothers and sisters, can a fig-tree bear olives, or a grapevine bear figs? Neither can a salt spring produce fresh water.'

We have probably all contradicted ourselves from time to time, or spoken critically soon after a moment of praise. We are all human, but inconsistency is not a holy habit. Allow me to illustrate with an incident from my large portfolio of awkward moments. One particularly stressful Sunday morning, our family experienced a less than holy conversation in the car on the way to church, with voices marginally raised and a smattering of interpersonal negativity (interpret as 'all-out war' if you don't recognise ironic nuance). Upon arrival into the church car park, a miracle of epic proportions occurred as we magically transformed into the McSmiley family, opening car doors for each other and preparing ourselves for friendly chatter with passers-by. Although we pulled off this relational U-turn, it is not something for which I am proud. It is not generally a good thing to pretend with people when we know something different is going on under the surface.

This link between who we are deep down and what we show to the world is a subject I explore more thoroughly in my book *Digging for Diamonds**. It seems to me that what we can't see, always shapes what we can see. What is hidden is always significant and will express itself somehow. As it says in Luke 6:45, 'A good man brings good things out of the good stored up in his heart, and an evil man brings evil things out of the evil stored up in his heart. For the mouth speaks what the heart is full of.' The external choices we make always begin with internal permission and the words we say don't appear in a vacuum. Bitter words come from a bitter heart and critical words come from a critical spirit. Hurt people will often say hurtful things. Likewise, grateful people tend to give thanks more readily and forgiven people often show forgiveness more easily.

So, if what we say is a symptom of who we really are, can we then diagnose our spiritual health by our choice of words? James seems to suggest it is possible. If a salt spring can't produce fresh water and a fig tree can't bear olives, then it is not likely that a bitter heart will authentically overflow with sweet words. Any discrepancy or inconsistency between who we are and what we say is therefore an unwelcome and inauthentic tension, which we should not learn to live with or accept. It *should* cause us discomfort. As we grow in self-awareness and surrender to God, what springs from our mouth will hopefully represent more of Christ at work in us.

Lord, forgive my inconsistency and my critical words. Create in me a clean heart that will overflow and represent You well. Holy Spirit, renew me daily as I pursue a consistent faith. Amen.

* Cathy Madavan, *Digging for Diamonds* (Milton Keynes: Authentic Media, 2015)

THE WISDOM OF HEAVEN

JAMES 3:13–18

'Who is wise and understanding among you? Let them show it by their good life, by deeds done in the humility that comes from wisdom. But if you harbour bitter envy and selfish ambition in your hearts, do not boast about it or deny the truth. Such "wisdom" does not come down from heaven but is earthly, unspiritual, demonic. For where you have envy and selfish ambition, there you find disorder and every evil practice'

But the wisdom that comes from heaven is first of all pure; then peace-loving, considerate, submissive, full of mercy and good fruit, impartial and sincere. Peacemakers who sow in peace reap a harvest of righteousness.'

James starts this section of his letter by asking, 'Who is wise and understanding among you?' A good question, I am sure you would agree. Am I wise or am I not? Do I have good understanding? Sometimes, maybe. In certain ways, possibly. But then, having asked his readers to consider themselves more deeply, James then clarifies his question by asking what kind of wisdom it is that we have – an earthly wisdom or a heavenly wisdom? One that reveals a root of selfish ambition, or one that reveals purity, peace, submission and good fruit? Now that really is a question worth asking, but potentially an uncomfortable one to answer.

It's likely that we've all met people in our churches, workplaces and families who have a powerful intellect, a quick tongue or a cleverness that seems very convincing and even 'wise', but who sometimes leave a trail of disruption and conflict in their wake. As a church leader, my husband occasionally receives 'feedback' by email where the sender writes convincingly of the need for change, but whose tone and methods leave much to be desired. They might be rigorous and they could even be right, but they are not always wise. James is clear that the truly smart people in life are those who build peace, and therefore harvest righteousness.

This very clear and repeated New Testament mandate to intentionally make peace, while simultaneously demonstrating mercy and even submission, needs to be emphasised. Now, I don't mean to suggest we all wear a respectable mask and side-step issues in a quest to be 'nice'. Avoiding difficulty is not always wise or a strategy for building lasting peace, and harvests very little either spiritually or relationally. No, James is calling us to pursue genuine unity as we purposefully sow seeds of accountability, reconciliation and restoration.

We are God's family, who are called to show the world that it is not always necessary to label each other, to gossip or to compete with our opinions. Wisdom should never be about our own self-promotion or being right at all costs. Certainly, we don't score any spiritual points by having the loudest voice or the most flamboyant vocabulary. Rather, we can demonstrate that it is possible to listen and love and to honestly grow closer together, even when we are different. We can deliberately hear from people who believe different things and show them respect. We can be sincere in our words and bring each other closer to Jesus by speaking truth with genuine love. That is heavenly wisdom.

Thank You, God, that You ask us to pursue unity not uniformity. You know that we are different but You ask us to be one in Christ. Make me a wise peacemaker today. Amen.

Loving

Loneliness can be overwhelming. Although being alone is not always a bad thing (I hear you, my introverted friends), being lonely is another deal altogether. People can feel lonely when stood in the middle of a crowd, or isolated when surrounded by work colleagues. Folk can feel disconnected even as they post inspirational pictures of their insta-glamourous life on social media. It's possible to feel incredibly alone inside a marriage. And let's get it out there: people can even feel like outsiders in church. It's worth saying again: people don't just need a friendly church – people need friends. Gleaming smiles from the welcome team are all well and good, but if all we see is a community that we do not feel part of, it merely makes us feel like retreating further.

Isolation and disconnection inevitably lead us towards further division and misunderstanding. But fortunately, there is an antidote to this tragic trajectory, and that is love. Purposeful, determined, selfless, kind, encouraging and challenging love. Love brings transformation to individuals and societies and it is supposed to be the hallmark of the people of God. Jesus, in His heartfelt prayer in John 17, declares that it is possible for Christians to be so totally devoted to one another and to Him that the world will know that He is the way, the truth and the life. Isn't that incredible? Jesus' words suggest that the greatest revival will happen when there is first a revival of love.

Loving each other is not mere mushy emotion, however. This is not about sentimental feelings or sending endless emojies with hearts for eyes. Loving people on purpose takes some serious commitment. God is very aware that we are all different (some of us are very different) but He still calls us to love each other, despite the obstacles to that goal. For example, there are people with whom we immediately click and who we love easily. My heart sings when I think of certain people. I look forward to being with them and blessing them however I can. Beyond that, I will happily enjoy spending time with most people, providing I can escape at some point. But then there are those I find more difficult: people who make all the right noises but who repeatedly make bad choices. People who are always late. People who are patronising or who leak negativity. People who never admit to having any problems. People who eat loudly. (Please, in the name of all that is good, just make it stop. And why would you *ever* eat crisps on trains?) I could go on. Let's admit it, it is not always easy to love those with whom we do not instinctively agree or like.

But then we consider Jesus, who had a definite habit of inviting difficult people into His orbit to love on purpose. He sat, at His final supper, loving people around the table who would disappoint Him and who had already betrayed Him. Not your average dinner party, then. Nobody was so poor or corrupt or difficult or disgraced that they were not welcomed by Jesus. And then, in a parable, He suggests that when the respectable folk don't accept His invitation, He joyfully invites whoever will come and *loves* being with them (Matt. 22:1–10). Friends, what if God celebrates when we deliberately love people who are different to us or difficult to like immediately? Don't we all deserve God's grace, after all? Aren't we all a bit difficult to love and less than perfect in all kinds of ways?

The problem is often that our own unfulfilled need for love prevents us from loving others. Our own lack of security can be a stumbling block as we get stuck in a loop of seeking approval or acceptance rather than being freed to love as Jesus loves. Many of us are still lonely and waiting for the kind of community, church or family who will express to us the kind of love that we so wish we had. We are still praying for that mentor, that special friend, that significant person or that group of buddies who would make life better.

I really do empathise. Mark and I have built our own family despite the context of a broken and distant extended family. It has not been easy. I intended to be a perfect wife but I got married at 20 and had no clue whatsoever; we have learned a lot of things, but mainly the hard way. Added to that, we are the pastor and wife, which doesn't naturally make us one of the gang when it comes to social invites (and means we are almost always busy anyway, which doesn't help). I've had my fair share of feeling isolated over the years.

So, what do we do when we don't live in a love surplus but we are still called to love? My considered opinion after years of thinking about this is to go back to the source of unconditional love and ask *Him* to fill our tank, and then we can step out and give to others what we wish we had ourselves. I believe that, with God's help, it is possible for us to build families and friendships and communities that bring life and love. We can purposefully create connections and encourage people wherever we go, investing in God's glorious Church to make her better and deliberately believing that there is beauty in every person. Let's be determined to break the chains of rejection and loneliness in us *and* others as we love on purpose with the love God gives us.

Mark and I decided years ago to be more proactive about this and began to deliberately host parties, to invite teams around for pudding nights (where they bring the puddings – yes, this is genius), and to involve people in the lives of our kids who could be like an extended family. As we have opened our doors (and our hearts) to others and as we have been vulnerable about our own needs, we have begun to reverse the isolation tide and, although there is much still to do, we believe that our home and our church will be places of loving community.

It is *only* God's unconditional love that recreates the foundation of our life in such a way that we can love others. We should still be wise about who we do life with; not everybody needs to be in our inner circle or to have access to us at all hours (even Jesus had boundaries) but we can always nurture a heart of compassion and a posture of welcome over defensiveness. Love consistently chooses to humbly consider others as even more significant than ourselves (Phil. 2) and treats them as if they are treasured by God – because they are. Then, as we give God's love away on purpose, we will not only receive more back ourselves than we could imagine but, equally important, we share His gift of unconditional love with a hurting world.

- How connected are you to God's unconditional love for you? If it is in the security of His love that we can love others, how might you know more of His presence and power in your life?

- What if on Sundays, everybody was the church welcome team? How can you make others feel truly welcome and connected into your church family?

- How connected do you feel to your church? Can you commit to a small group or a team? Could you plan a bank holiday walk or create an event on Facebook? How can you create more meaningful relationships?

- Could you invite some people to your home (get them to bring food if you hate cooking)? Try including somebody who isn't already a friend. Ask God to help you to welcome them and love them on purpose.

God as a kind of adultery (v4). A husband or wife doesn't need to feel possessive if their spouse has an innocent conversation or friendship with somebody, but they would be entitled to feel jealous if somebody tried to seduce their spouse, leading them away from their covenant relationship. The problem we face is that we are far less faithful towards God than He is to us.

We must be purposeful about devoting ourselves to our relationship with God. Frequently and without thought, we place other ambitions in front of Him. We talk to other people more than we talk to Him. We make other things a priority in the calendar while our quiet times, Sundays and serving become less of a commitment. And yet He is our first love and our relationship with Him will last for eternity. He deserves our devotion and our attention. We simply can't be both seduced by the world and in love with Jesus, as James reminds us here.

Thankfully, the Spirit will lead us back home to our Father, who will always welcome us with open arms. He dwells in us and invites us to dwell in Him. Let's choose again to make ourselves completely at home with our loving God, committed to living faithfully and joyfully for Him and His purposes alone.

Lord, forgive my unfaithfulness towards You. Thank You that You are so zealous about Your people and that You love me so unconditionally. I wholeheartedly give myself back to You today. Amen.

GREATER GRACE

JAMES 4:6-10

'But he gives us more grace. That is why Scripture says: "God opposes the proud but shows favour to the humble." **Submit yourselves, then, to God. Resist the devil, and he will flee from you. Come near to God and he will come near to you.** *Wash your hands, you sinners, and purify your hearts, you double-minded. Grieve, mourn and wail. Change your laughter to mourning and your joy to gloom. Humble yourselves before the Lord, and he will lift you up.'*

In the days of yore, before email and digital messages infiltrated modern life, I used to receive many more handwritten letters in the post. These days, it is a rare and therefore exciting moment to open a letter that isn't junk mail with my address penned by hand on the front. My favourite envelopes however, are the ones that contain an invitation inside, asking us to attend a wedding or a special celebration of some kind, with a request to RSVP ASAP to the good news.

Opening today's portion of James' letter, we find it contains some wonderful news and an invitation inside for us. Having previously been reminded of our fickle nature as well as repeatedly asked to choose our allegiance and to commit to it (in many ways, the theme of the whole letter), James now pauses to remind us of some very good news indeed: there is always more grace.

This is a moment to savour. Whatever mistakes we make and however distracted we may become, there is always a way back to God. He always has more than enough grace to outweigh our misdemeanours. As we humble ourselves before Him again, He pours out His grace anew and we are reconciled to our maker. Thanks to Jesus, we are invited into the throne room of God knowing that His mercy and forgiveness are never in doubt.

But that undeniably good news and accompanying invitation require a response from us. We are effectively being asked to RSVP ASAP. God's lavish grace isn't given to us so that we can opt out and be excused from taking part in His plans for our life. Why would we ignore such a wonderful request to draw near to God when He has provided a way for us to come into His presence? We need to accept and take our place at the table He has prepared for us.

James says that our RSVP to God is to actively 'submit' and 'resist' (v7). We are called both to surrender ourselves again to God and to defend ourselves from the pressure of the world and the enemy. As we deploy this double-pronged strategy we will know His strength, and we will come closer to God, who, in turn comes closer to us. What a fantastic promise and a glorious outcome.

The invitation still stands for us today: God asks us to follow Him closely and to know His presence – but our response is still required. Thank God that as we humble ourselves there is always more than enough grace to cover us, and a divine strategy that equips us to stand firm in our faith.

Thank You, Lord, for Your amazing invitation of grace. I choose to respond today by intentionally submitting to You and resisting the enemy. Lift me up Lord, and draw me close to You again. Amen.

LIFTING OTHERS UP

JAMES 4:11-12

'Brothers and sisters, do not slander one another. Anyone who speaks against a brother or sister or judges them speaks against the law and judges it.
When you judge the law, you are not keeping it, but sitting in judgment on it. There is only one Lawgiver and Judge, the one who is able to save and destroy. But you—who are you to judge your neighbour?'

Life as a freelancer has plenty of benefits as well as frustrations, but one drawback is never knowing what to say when people ask the inevitable question, 'What is it that you do?' Since I don't work for an organisation or have a title, a few years ago, I decided to give myself a secret unofficial position. I chose the lofty title of 'Chief Cheerleader' (although to clarify, this is without pom-poms) with a job description that revolves around intentionally encouraging people and choosing language that will show my appreciation of others. This means that wherever I am, in the supermarket, online or on a stage; whatever I am writing; whoever I am speaking to; I hope to be somebody who leaves a person feeling or doing better because of our time together.

There is something very powerful about our choice of language. James asks his fellow believers to deliberately select their words. It's tempting to fall into slander, gossip or 'sharing for prayer' what is not ours to share at all. We can all so easily comment on the parenting techniques, attitudes, inefficiency or lack of generosity in others, when we don't know the whole picture. Perhaps we do it to make ourselves feel or look better, but it is worth asking ourselves whether we would speak differently if the person was sat in front of us.

There is no shortage of criticism in the world. In fact, negativity is like an epidemic and is highly contagious. You don't need any skill, training or insight to spot a problem or to share a shortcoming. But encouragement is something we choose. We give respect and appreciate on purpose. In Ephesians 4:29, Paul encourages us to 'not let any unwholesome talk come out of your mouths, but only what is helpful for building others up according to their needs, that it may benefit those who listen.'

And who are we to judge anyway, asks James? Judging others is a kind of arrogance that puts us above another person, dishonouring them in the process. James reminds us that taking a superior position is the very antithesis of the way of Jesus, who deliberately chose words and actions that honoured the least and questioned those with influence.

Today, the words you speak could be *exactly* what somebody's weary soul needs to hear. As you send that encouraging text or write that letter of appreciation, you resist tearing down, and build somebody up instead. It doesn't take a lot to see the good in others and to then speak it out as you encourage what you see, but you'll be amazed at the results.

I worship You, Lord Jesus, and thank You for Your words of hope and life. Help me to take every opportunity to encourage rather than judge. Give me words to lift somebody up today. Amen.

A DISAPPEARING MIST

JAMES 4:13-17

'Now listen, you who say, "Today or tomorrow we will go to this or that city, spend a year there, carry on business and make money." **Why, you do not even know what will happen tomorrow. What is your life? You are a mist that appears for a little while and then vanishes.** Instead, you ought to say, "If it is the Lord's will, we will live and do this or that." As it is, you boast in your arrogant schemes. All such boasting is evil. If anyone, then, knows the good they ought to do and doesn't do it, it is sin for them.'

Following on from yesterday, the next personal challenge James presents to us is the temptation to believe we are totally in control of our own lives. If judging others is a more obvious kind of arrogance, this is a subtler but still significant lack of humility. This belief convinces us that we are the ultimate deciders of our own destiny and that if we plan it, we will succeed in it. We speak as if we are the masters of our future, when life, like the morning mist, is more fragile than we may care to admit. We might outwardly agree that God is in control, but the reality is that we'd like to hold tightly onto the reins of our life ourselves, and that is what James is challenging here.

Now, it is not a bad thing to live with confidence and it is good to follow a dream. It is sensible to have goals and ticking off a decent to-do list gives some of us huge pleasure (my list-addiction is well documented). Living life 'on accident' rather than on purpose can result in a lack of any direction or focus, so planning is necessary. But let's be aware of the temptation to create plans for our lives according to our own will and purposes. Everything we do should be surrendered to God,

but also has the potential to corrode our hearts.

Jesus also taught regularly about the power of our possessions. In fact, He talked more about how we handle our material wealth than He did about prayer. This is because our attitudes towards what we own and towards selfless sacrifice reveal a lot about who is in control of our life. Affluence can always easily open a door to arrogance, and power is always a challenge to steward well. God cares deeply about our character and is concerned about the ethics of how we earn, the impact of money on our attitudes, and the dangers of indulgence that might distract us or lead us away from our faith.

The question is this: do we own our stuff, or does our stuff own us? Whatever our income, do we spend more time thinking about our lifestyle, or about how to love God and others? We don't need to feel embarrassed if we are blessed in financial terms, and we don't need to feel less significant if we have less, but we can all use our resources wisely, to extend God's kingdom and to live loving and generous lives. Every one of us can resolve to share what we have and to create budgets that bless God, build His Church and serve the poor. If we can withstand the temptation to continually overindulge, our resources are a wonderful tool with huge potential to give God glory and to change lives. Let's offer back to Him all that He has so generously given to us.

Thank You, Lord, for every material blessing. I pray for all who live with so much less that I do today. Help me to serve You more than money, to know my worth is found in You and to live a generous life. Amen.

Growing

I am dealing with personal trauma. There I was getting on with life and then BAM! Suddenly I realised I had crossed a threshold and stopped being young. Nobody prepared me for this (apart from the subtle hints from my increasing waistline, maybe).

The realisation set in fully this year when I was speaking at a wonderful conference for women in Denmark. On the second morning, the music pumped up and a fitness instructor bounced onto the stage and encouraged us all to hit the floor to do the plank with one hand behind our backs. I laughed loudly and looked around for someone to roll my eyes to and give some 'yeah, as if' non-verbal communication. However, everybody was already laid horizontal, getting friendly with the floorboards. I couldn't believe it. It would take a winch and a team of physiotherapists for me to pull off that move.

Then later, just as I had recovered my composure, one of the conference organisers thanked me for my teaching and shared that they had deliberately invited me as an older, more mature woman to speak into their lives. I smiled and nodded in a sage-like manner but everything in me was screaming, 'I am in my mid-forties for goodness sake! I am not wearing surgical stockings or subscribing to *Reader's Digest* just yet!'

It might have come as unwelcome news that I am now regarded as 'mature' but I can't help but be impressed by those (OK, young) Danish women. They knew that they

ON PURPOSE

needed help to tackle the challenges they face at their time of life and so they deliberately put themselves in front of somebody who had already fought some of their battles. Similarly, I am always greatly encouraged as I coach less experienced preachers or leaders who are open and willing to receive guidance and feedback. It takes some vulnerability and courage to grow on purpose by looking for input from others.

We are never too young or too old to learn and develop, but growth is not inevitable. All of us can get fixed in our thinking in different areas. It is only as we challenge these mental ruts and ask God for fresh thinking that we can imagine a new path ahead. As we dare to dream and purposefully set ourselves some development goals, we begin to create some new momentum. All of us have areas in our relationships, careers or ministries where we have begun to believe that nothing will happen or that progress has stalled for good. But surely an inner renewal is possible with God's help?

A helpful habit for me has been to regularly list different areas of my life and to pray about where I need to stretch again. Where do I need to purposefully grow? What areas would benefit hugely from a chat with an inspiring friend, pastor or a coach? Are there some obstacles that are so big that I need some help to stop me stalling? Then, after praying, consulting, thinking and often writing some things down, I can plan some next steps to help me start moving in the right direction again. It's amazing to read back and to see how things do shift and change when I purposefully pursue growth.

Some of us just need to get moving again and then see where that leads. I won't ever forget somebody once saying to me, 'It is easier for God to steer a moving car'. Maybe you need to invest in your gifts, sign up for that class, get yourself to that conference or build that business. Perhaps it is time to say yes to that serving opportunity or to meeting up with that person. Every now and then we need to grab or create an opportunity, knowing that God probably put the dream in our heart to start with. Let's not sit waiting for somebody else to give us permission or to open the right doors. That might happen, but it might not. God gives us our permission and He loves it when we willingly follow Him into new faith adventures.

A reality check might be in order here, however. The sobering truth is that we often learn and grow more in the hard times than we do in the easy times. If there is an easier route to maturity, gratitude and wisdom other than through suffering, experience or endurance, it hasn't been found yet. Just as you get stronger in the gym when your muscles push against resistance, so we get internally stronger as we push through life's challenges. Resilience requires resistance but it means facing the pressure and not running away. Paul, in Romans 5:3–5 says, 'Not only so, but we also glory in our sufferings, because we know that suffering produces perseverance; perseverance, character; and character, hope. And hope does not put us to shame, because God's love has been poured out into our hearts through the Holy Spirit.'

We would all prefer to avoid pain, wouldn't we? Suffering is not on my top list of things to do, ever. Failing and disappointing people are also equally unpalatable prospects. We would like things to go right, for people to love us and to be as comfortable as possible, if you please. But Paul suggests that there is a glory to what God accomplishes in us through life's trials, including knowing more of God's love and hope, which is surely our heart's desire. It's hard to accept, but there is often a season of pruning *before* a season of growing – it's just that we rarely welcome the secateurs.

I wonder how many times over the years I have failed to grow stronger, wiser or more experienced because of anxiety about failing or the fear of discomfort. I wonder how often I have not invested more commitment or energy, because the going has got tough or the pruning has felt brutal. The alternative to growth, though, is settling and stagnating and accepting a flabby, stunted version of who I might be, which, for me, has become an even more uncomfortable proposition than failing to try.

Those Danish women were right about some things then, darn it. You do eventually get a better grip on what matters, as you get older. You are not so dazzled by the apparent success of others that you feel inadequate in comparison. You don't get quite so crushed by criticism or cynicism. In my twenties, it was harder to genuinely celebrate the achievements of others because I hadn't found my own place of peace. Now, I honestly get as much pleasure from seeing those I mentor, parent, facilitate or lead flourish and grow, as I do when I jump a new hurdle or learn something new myself. Their growing doesn't threaten me anymore – it thrills me.

Our own accumulated wisdom, gleaned as we have navigated various mountains and valleys, can be turned outwards and used to bless and encourage others to grow stronger. Yes, we will all have a few regrets, but we have learned some useful stuff along the way. And while we are far from perfect, God hasn't finished with us yet either. Life goes too quickly to settle for less than we know God wants for us. So, whatever our age and circumstances, it may well be time to ask God for another season of growing on purpose.

- **Acknowledge any areas where there are limitations, challenges and obstacles. Ask for God's strength where you feel tired, for His renewal of hope where you feel disappointed and for His clarity and wisdom where you feel confused.**

- **List some different areas of life (eg faith, family, giving, serving, work, health, prayer, friendship, personal development, fun) and honestly assess where you are growing and where you have got a little stuck.**

- What steps will you take next to keep growing in each area of your life?

- Who could you speak to if you need help or accountability as you build momentum in certain areas?

- Could you also journal or write down some unfulfilled dreams, desires, prayers or promises that you long to see bear fruit in your life?

- How can you use your own experience to help others to grow? Where can you teach, encourage, cheer on, mentor or guide those who need support?

WAITING WELL

JAMES 5:7-9

'Be patient, then, brothers and sisters, until the Lord's coming. **See how the farmer waits for the land to yield its valuable crop, patiently waiting for the autumn and spring rains. You too, be patient and stand firm, because the Lord's coming is near.** Don't grumble against one another, brothers and sisters, or you will be judged. The Judge is standing at the door!'

If you have ever spent hours sat in a waiting room, twiddling your thumbs as you prepare yourself for an appointment with a dentist or doctor, I empathise. There have been a few occasions recently where, sat in a hospital waiting room, I have memorised every badly designed poster on the wall and then created a fictional back story for every person sat on the uncomfortable plastic chairs nearby. Waiting is often very frustrating.

But how we deal with waiting is important. This is because all of us, for different reasons in different seasons, will feel like we are caught in a holding pattern in an area of our life – say a relationship, a ministry, a job or a particular personal challenge. Perhaps even now you are waiting for news, for feedback, for a baby, for an answer, for exam results or for some new momentum in a specific area that feels a little bit stuck. Learning to wait well is the art of trusting God more fully.

Actually, we are all living in this in-between zone often described as the 'now but not yet'. We believe the kingdom of God exists in the world, and that we are living by the Spirit, but we are not yet living in the fullness of that kingdom as we are waiting for the final glorious return of Jesus. For now, believers are called to expectantly share the good news, to serve the poor, to build communities and to love each other beautifully as Christ loved us.

But waiting well requires trust and endurance, particularly when we come under pressure. James' wise advice is as relevant to us now as it was then: he says to stand firm and to be patient, believing there is a light at the end of the tunnel. Every one of us must guard ourselves against disappointment and bitterness as we wait, trusting His promises and His truth. But also, James says, as we wait we should cut out the grumbling and gossiping about each other. It doesn't help, it doesn't honour God and He really doesn't like it. You have to love James' straightforward but pertinent advice.

Just as a farmer waits for seeds to germinate and grow, we are all expected to wait patiently for new life and hope, knowing it is on its way. As we faithfully tend the ground we have been given and wait with purposeful perseverance, we do it together and with God, believing that a breakthrough is coming soon.

Lord, I give You the areas where I am waiting today. Help me to wait on You and to wait well. Keep my spirit sweet and my hope alive as I live in the present, trusting You for the future. Amen.

YOU ARE NOT ALONE

JAMES 5:10–11

'Brothers and sisters, as an example of patience in the face of suffering, take the prophets who spoke in the name of the Lord. **As you know, we count as blessed those who have persevered. You have heard of Job's perseverance and have seen what the Lord finally brought about. The Lord is full of compassion and mercy.'**

As I write, the faces of some special friends come to mind. Over the past few years these friends have experienced a series of tragedies in quick succession. They have encountered loss, confusion and practical complications beyond what most of us could imagine, let alone handle. Every time they have recalibrated a little, another obstacle or heartbreak has emerged for them to navigate. However, even though they might have every reason to rant and rage, they have consistently spoken of God's compassion and mercy amidst it all. They have been honest about the pain, and frank about the cost, but they have been dependent upon God to keep them afloat when they so easily could have sunk.

Ask yourself how the everyday, ordinary Christian heroes you know have impacted your faith. There are so many courageous people who, despite having no choice in the matter, have faced suffering or enormous challenges with the kind of faith and peace that leave us feeling inspired and humbled.

This is the reason James asks his fellow believers to recall the lives of the prophets and Job who had gone before them. We all need examples of those who have run the race well before us. At some point, we all get consumed with our own troubles and think we are the only ones who have ever faced our situation. We forget that others have travelled a similar road, and that we are rarely alone. Of course, all pain is personalised and nobody has ever walked in your exact shoes, but there is power in community and solidarity in suffering where empathy flows more easily.

And guess what? Just as others have been an example to us, so God can use our challenges too. It says in 2 Corinthians 1:4 that God 'comforts us in all our troubles, so that we can comfort those in any trouble with the comfort we ourselves receive from God'. We can find purpose in our pain, no matter how unwelcome it is. God doesn't ever waste anything, and our experience might be the hope that somebody else needs as they pass through their own murky waters. The question is whether we can see the compassion of God at work clearly enough to be able to share it with others. Let's not shut ourselves off from our heavenly Father when we need Him the most. He can cope with hearing your disappointment, but He will also meet you in it and even use it for His glory – if you let Him.

Thank You, Lord, for those who have followed You against the odds. Thank You for Jesus, who suffered so greatly and who brings us hope. I give You the dark and chaotic places of my life and ask You to let there be light. Amen.

CONSISTENT AND CLEAR

JAMES 5:12

'Above all, my brothers and sisters, do not swear – not by heaven or by earth or by anything else. All you need to say is a simple "Yes" or "No."' Otherwise you will be condemned.'

One of the best pieces of parenting advice I was given when my children were young was, 'Say what you mean, and mean what you say'. Children need to know that you are consistent and will follow through on your promises and your threats. There is absolutely no point saying to a tantruming 'threenager' that you will leave the park unless they calm down if you have no intention of leaving the park. If you have arranged to meet somebody else there, then that clever toddler brain knows full well that you are going nowhere. On with the tantrum, then. Similarly, if you promise to take a child to breakfast as a reward for working hard and you don't follow through because of your own busyness or tiredness, your failure to deliver on that promise will have a detrimental effect. That child will inevitably interpret your actions as saying that other things are more important than they are. None of us are perfect (I have a list of regrets a mile long), and sometimes circumstances conspire against us, but ideally when we say it, we should mean it.

Consistency and clarity are far from being just parenting issues, of course. We all know how it feels when people flannel us instead of telling us the truth. We all know what empty threats and broken promises look like, and we recognise people who are trying to distort the facts to fit their purposes. Most of us have shaken our heads in disbelief as we have watched certain politicians being interviewed who, in their desperate attempts to avoid promising anything too definite or incriminating themselves, have therefore said nothing of substance at all.

James' instructions to his fellow believers are so helpful to us in a culture of spin. As we are waiting, persevering and following faithfully, we should not get frustrated, lose focus or distort reality to convince others of our intentions. We don't need to twist truth, fudge facts or overpromise and under-deliver. We only ever need to be honest and straightforward: saying what we mean and meaning what we say. People trust us when we follow through on our 'yes' and stand firm on our 'no'.

This doesn't mean being inflexible or resistant to new information. Rather, we should be secure enough to follow through on our commitments and to be honest about our difficulties. Our character should demonstrate the kind of authentic and transparent consistency that is becoming an increasingly rare commodity today. What an opportunity for the Church to demonstrate what truly trustworthy relationships can look like.

Thank You, Lord, that You are the way, the truth and the life. May Your people be a transparent and trustworthy reflection of Your character. Make us more consistently like You, we pray. Amen.

POWER-ASSISTED LIVING

JAMES 5:13–18

'Is anyone among you in trouble? Let them pray. Is anyone happy? Let them sing songs of praise. Is anyone among you sick? Let them call the elders of the church to pray over them and anoint them with oil in the name of the Lord. And the prayer offered in faith will make the sick person well; the Lord will raise them up. If they have sinned, they will be forgiven. **Therefore confess your sins to each other and pray for each other so that you may be healed. The prayer of a righteous person is powerful and effective.'**

Elijah was a human being, even as we are. He prayed earnestly that it would not rain, and it did not rain on the land for three and a half years. Again he prayed, and the heavens gave rain, and the earth produced its crops.'

For a while, when my car was poorly last year, I had to drive a much older vehicle that lacked any mod-cons at all such as power steering, electric windows or decent heating. Although I don't usually drive anything new or particularly flashy, I had honestly forgotten what cars used to be like. It felt like driving a small tank! But if driving without power-assisted steering is arduous, then living without the assistance of God's power is exhausting. It's just not how we are designed to function.

Towards the end of his letter, James goes back to the theme he started with at the beginning – faith-filled prayer. In these verses, we get the distinct impression that prayer should permeate everything we do. Whether we are happy, sick, weighed down by guilt or just plain tired, we can respond with prayers of praise, with requests or with confession.

This is so encouraging. Prayer has the power to be a dynamic living conversation with God that connects us continually and holistically with our maker. He *longs* for the restoration of our mind, body and soul and wants us to bring all things to Him. Our creator's desire is to recreate His world, to make all things new, and He wants us to participate with Him on His mission. What a privilege prayer is!

I recently visited a family with my daughter and as we shared some of the challenges we are currently facing, they immediately suggested that we stop and pray together. As we prayed, we received some real insight and encouragement about the path ahead. Prayer releases God's potential in us and through us. As we pray alone or together, we lift each other up, we see God at work and we grow in faith and maturity as we witness what power-assisted living looks like.

Most of us occasionally default back to trying to steer our own life, crunching through the gears ourselves, carrying our own weight in our own strength. All of us sometimes feel guilty, knowing we fail to make prayer the priority it should be in our busy diaries. But James is reminding us again that life is not supposed to be like driving an ancient vehicle that trudges around life's corners without any power. Not at all.

Maybe today is the day for a spiritual MOT, as it were. It's always a good time to recalibrate and to remember that living on purpose with God is at the heart of everything we do. As we pray in faith, God will raise us up and set us free to live for Him.

Lord, as I discover more about You and Your purposes in prayer, please come and fill me with Your Holy Spirit. Bless Your people with Your power, peace and presence as we pray in faith together. Amen.

BRINGING PEOPLE HOME

JAMES 5:19–20

'My brothers and sisters, if one of you should wander from the truth and someone should bring that person back, remember this: **Whoever turns a sinner from the error of their way will save them from death and cover over a multitude of sins.'**

It is so exciting when a person comes through the front door of a church and finds faith for the first time. One of the undisputed highlights of our church's year is the baptism service, where we hear the testimony of new believers who have turned from their old hopelessness towards the acceptance and forgiveness of Christ. Every one of us wants to celebrate and welcome a new member into God's family.

But as well as having a front door, every church also has a back door. This is the exit that a person drifts quietly through without any fanfare or announcement. Perhaps that discouraged disciple has suffered disappointment or lived with lingering doubts. They may feel let down or burdened with unanswered prayer or maybe, having made one compromise too many, they no longer feel comfortable in the house of God.

Time and time again James reminds us, as he does at the close of this letter, that we are brothers and sisters. We are not mere church attenders or members of a club; we are a family. We are not consumers or service-providers; we are a family. When we love each other with that kind of purpose and perseverance, we will care as much when people are headed for the back door as we did when they first came through the front door.

Clearly, it will take commitment, prayer and some serious courage to lovingly steer people back to Jesus, but let's remember that as we do, James says that we are effectively saving their life. The Good Shepherd has asked us all to look after His flock. Just as a sheep won't get to its destination by accident, so people often need leading and loving on purpose. We are all responsible for actively supporting each other as we would our own siblings or children – helping and encouraging them towards what is best for them. The next generation particularly need role models and friends if we want them to keep going in a world that screams at them to give up. In the Church family, every member is needed to keep following and to lovingly step out and fulfil God's glorious purposes.

And then, as we welcome brothers and sisters back into the family, we joyfully take our place at the table together, knowing that our heavenly Father, who loves His prodigal children, throws a party in their honour. How wonderful. We are *all* invited and welcomed into our Father's house and He doesn't want anybody to leave early or to miss out on His never-ending grace and love.

Thank You, God that You commission me to love others and to lead them to Christ. Lord, show me those who are heading for the front door and the back door so that I might help and encourage their journey of faith in Your family. Amen.

THE BEGINNING OF WISDOM

PROVERBS 9:10-11

'The fear of the LORD is the beginning of wisdom, and knowledge of the Holy One is understanding. For through wisdom your days will be many, and years will be added to your life.'

The book of James really is a rich treasure trove of axioms, proverbs, pictures and illustrations all shared by a practical pastor who knew Jesus intimately. It can also be, as we have discovered, a rather challenging read. James was respected enough to be extremely direct with his brothers and sisters, who knew how much he cared for them. Perhaps like me, you could almost hear the urgency in his voice as he appealed to them to guard their motives, to be humble, to show self-control, to care for the poor and to persevere. But also, you could sense his love (and maybe frustration) for this young church because he *wholeheartedly* believed that making wise choices and living on purpose would prevent them from falling into harm and would keep their faith alive.

I am quite sure that throughout the ages, many church leaders, parents, and friends who care deeply about discipleship have empathised with James' desire to keep his flock on track. Too many Christians have fooled themselves with inferior wisdom or received enough religion to feel guilty, but not enough of God to experience His unconditional love. Heavenly wisdom and understanding always adds to our life and 'the fear of the Lord is the beginning of wisdom'. As we respect God and put Him back in His rightful place, then we are motivated to deploy Scripture's practical instructions and to respond to correction as well.

James would never want us to just discover the truth though, he would want us to fully live it out. As the evangelist D.L. Moody famously said, 'The Bible was not given for our information but for our transformation.' Or as James himself wrote in 1:22, 'Do not merely listen to the word... Do what it says.' So, as we consider his teaching the question is: how do we move beyond hearing to action? Maybe ask yourself again what you need to start or stop doing. What do you need to believe more or stop believing? What ministry or relationship needs more investment? What attitude or habit needs some more attention?

Now is the time for each of us to move from existing to living more purposefully. None of us benefits from an unintentional life that bumps along, simply reacting to circumstances. With God's help, you and I get to sign up for the adventure of a holy, brave and persistent life that will change us and change the world through us. Let's believe it and live it on purpose.

As I pause and reflect, Lord Jesus, show me again where I have drifted and what I might need to adjust to live faithfully as Your disciple. What areas might need more prayer and attention and how should I proceed? How can I step up and step out again more fully for you? Holy Spirit, guide me, shape me and use me to bring transformation for your glory.

Thank You, God, that I do not need to settle for paddling in the shallows of Your love. Help me to understand the depths of Your wisdom but also to purposefully live it out for You. Fill me with Your Spirit again, I pray. Amen.

THANK YOU

I am indebted to so many people for making this journey through James possible. Firstly, a huge thanks to Lynette Brooks, Dave Ramsay and the whole CWR team whose unfailing encouragement, imagination, pep talks and willingness to flex on multiple deadlines (sorry!) has resulted in such a wonderful partnership. I'm grateful for all that you do – and for all that you are.

Thank you also to Krish Kandiah, Malcolm and Debbie Duncan, Cris Rogers, Rob Parsons, Sheridan Voysey, Jen Baker, Amy Boucher Pye and all my other online and offline writing buddies who have kept this show on the road in recent days. Thanks for your honesty, wisdom and insight.

And since we're at it, thank you to every person who has continued to encourage me in my ministry – it means more than you know. To be able to speak and write about the Christian faith is a privilege and meeting so many inspirational people is a constant blessing. Of course, a life in ministry is not without its challenges, but for the most part it has been amazing and I'm very grateful.

Also by Cathy Madavan

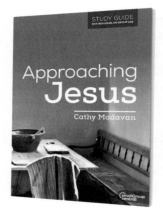

Take a look through the eyes of people who approached Jesus in the Gospel of Matthew, including the Pharisees, a desperate father, Peter and Judas. This six-week study guide is designed to help you or your small group learn more about who Jesus is today, and apply it to your own life.
ISBN: 978-1-78259-737-7

More on the book of James

This seven-week study, ideal for both individual and small group use, will challenge you to live your life as God intended. James confronts, challenges and calls us to be committed to not only hearing the Word, but to do what it says.
Author: Trevor J. Partridge
ISBN: 978-1-85345-293-2

To find out more about these resources (and the whole *Cover to Cover* Bible Study series) including current prices and ordering information, visit **www.cwr.org.uk/shop** or call **01252 784700**.
Also available in Christian bookshops.

Be inspired by God.
Every day.

Confidently face life's challenges by equipping yourself daily with God's Word. There is something for everyone...

Every Day with Jesus

Selwyn Hughes' renowned writing is updated by Mick Brooks into these trusted and popular notes.

Life Every Day

Jeff Lucas helps apply the Bible to daily life through his trademark humour and insight.

Inspiring Women Every Day

Encouragement, uplifting scriptures and insightful daily thoughts for women.

The Manual

Straight-talking guides to help men walk daily with God. Written by Carl Beech.

To find out more about all our daily Bible reading notes, or to take out a subscription, visit **www.cwr.org.uk/biblenotes** or call 01252 784700.
Also available in Christian bookshops.

 Printed format   Large print format   Email format   Ebook format

Discover more about CWR, our ministry, training and all our resources at www.cwr.org.uk

Courses and seminar

Waverley Abbey Colleg

Publishing and medi

Conference facilitie

Transforming lives

CWR's vision is to enable people to experience person transformation through applying God's Word to their lives and relationships.

Our Bible-based training and resources help people around the world to:
· Grow in their walk with God
· Understand and apply Scripture to their lives
· Resource themselves and their church
· Develop pastoral care and counselling skills
· Train for leadership
· Strengthen relationships, marriage and family life
  and much more.

Our insightful writers provide daily Bible reading note and other resources for all ages, and our experienced course designers and presenters have gained an international reputation for excellence and effectiveness.

CWR's Training and Conference Centre in Surrey, England, provides excellent facilities in idyllic settings ideal for both learning and spiritual refreshment.

CWR Applying God's Word
to everyday life and relationships

CWR, Waverley Abbey House,
Waverley Lane, Farnham,
Surrey GU9 8EP, UK

Telephone: **+44 (0)1252 784700**
Email: **info@cwr.org.uk**
Website: **www.cwr.org.uk**

Registered Charity No. 294387
Company Registration No. 1990308